HOW T SIDELOAD APPS INTO YOUR KINDLE FIRE

A Complete Guide on How sideload Apps into Kindle Devices in less than 5 Minutes for Beginners to Pro.

BY

NEWMAN ALEX
Copyright©2017

COPY RIGHT

Newman Alex

TABLE OF CONTENT

CHAPTER 1

INTRODUCTION

Present times, Amazons kindle fire stage of performance occur in a walled garden of sort.

Amazon has apps for android device in store to always make apps available for kindle fire list.

The apps in store for android don't always have similar or specific type as Google play .

Due to the outcome you'll keep looking for things and never finding it, and not just indistinct apps either, on the other hand well know apps like the android version of Google chrome browser.

You can create important alteration or change by installing Google play on your kindle fire, but is disorganized, it requires support, and it can reject you Amazon Assurance. You can relish alternative apps on your device by side loading them you can download them and installing them manually from a reliable source, also you can extract from another android devices and install them. We will educate you on both techniques. By using a kindle fire HDX to educate, even though individual format may be in poles part location on kindle fires, the procedures still works on all kindle fire devices {you will have to stick around in the settings menu for some time.

It is one important pitfall to side load applications outside the administration of an appstore application NOTE that applications Google play or Amazons apps for Android. Automatically you will lose updates. it is important to be watchful when side loading   apps that a security focused application that should be up to date, I advise you to keep an eye on the application and make sure that the updates are been sideloading when necessary.

CHAPTER 2

GET YOUR KINDLE FIRE READ

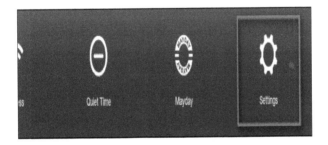

First of all prepare you kindle fire to accept them before sideloading apps, also set up a file manager and directory to enable working with the side loaded apps simple.

Move to the down top navigation bar click on settings look for the application menu.

The application menu, located at the top you'll find the unknown sources toggle.

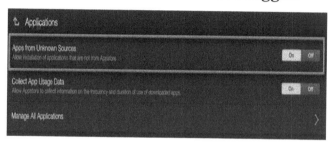

Switch the settings to on. This settings needs
to remain long in the on state as you're sideloading apps. I advice turning it off when you are not actively sideloading apps to high up security and avoid installation of unwanted or dangerous software.
When you've turned unknown source on, open the apps for android applications and search for ES file explorer.

Newman Alex

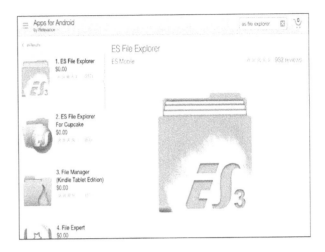

ES file explorer is well supported, easy to use and free.
Create a folder in the root of the Kindle's internal storage either by running ES file explorer and tapping the new button at the bottom to create a new folder you can also connect the kindle to your PC with a USB cable and creating folder with your operating system file explorer, either you create a folder/sideload apps/in the root like that.

The folder will serve as store for incoming APK files.

CHAPTER THREE

INSTALLATION OF ANDROID APPS YOU HAVE DOWNLOADED

APK file you can't find in the apps for Android store, the desktop manager that permits you to manage your installed apps through your PC you won't be able to find snapPea in the apps for android store, you can only download the APK directly from snapPea .

When using the snapPea app, you can use any APK you have downloaded from a reliable source. You have to copy the APK file to the sideloaded apps, folder and lunch ES Explorer on your kindle fire.

Move to sideload apps and your APK file will display, tap on it to launch into Android installation process.

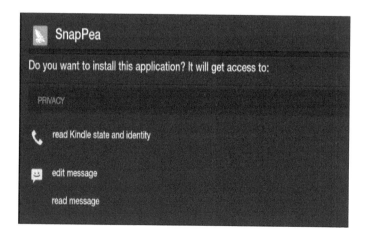

It will display the accessibility of the app and modify, it will be displayed at the bottom of the screen to finish the application permissions after reviewing. When done the app will you can be able click open.

Perfect! Your app is now installed on your kindle fire you don't need to depend on Amazon's appstore.

CHAPTER 4

INSTALATION OF APP FROM GOOGLE PLAY STORE

Installing apps you have downloaded to your android device, or have not downloaded? Don't worry we got your back.
Installation of apps from Google play store has it's own steps which can be completed either from web or from your device.

The initial technique depends on using Google chrome to download the APK files from the Google play stores web interface we tutored you how to use the APK Downloader to siphon apps right out of the store.

If you remove the extra steps in the APK Downloader guide you have to find a Google play ID from a donor device also you can lift the apps off your existing device. Its been done when we need a benchmark application that was not at reach in the apps for android store but was available in the play store.

The objective of this technique, app Backup & Restore on your android once installed, to backup apps on your device for transfer to your kindle fire simply run the app backup and check. Press the backup button at the bottom.

It will be stored in the directory and specified by App Backup(in our case, storage/sdcard0/app-backup Restore/,check the application settings to view what your storage directory is.) after been backed up, you simply need to mount your device on your computer.

Even if you downloaded them with Google pay store or you copied with APP Backup, you now have the APK file and copy it /sideloaded APPS/ folder on your kindle fire. Now repeat the format I outlined in the first part of the guild to install the APK file and you are in business. Now here's Google chrome installed on our kindle fire HDX.

Aside from the not-quite-Retina-quality display icon, the browser is indistinguishable from another other native app and works just as well on our Kindle HDX as it does on all our other Android devices. Success

With a little patience and a work around or two up your sleeve, you can easily get the apps you want on your Kindle Fire, whether or not Amazon ever gets around to putting them in the Apps for Android store.

THE END

Newman Alex

Newman Alex

Newman Alex

Newman Alex